Cooking with

Soulfult

Table of Contents

I. Meats

8

II. Side Dishes

Table of Contents

Meats

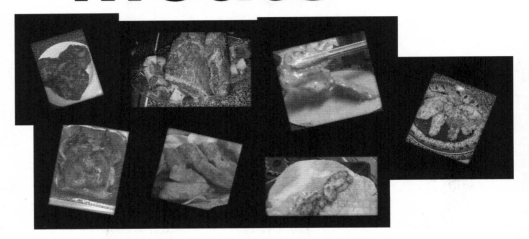

Roasted Chicken

You will need

A whole Chicken, a whole lemon, fresh thyme, fresh garlic, 1 whole onion, 1 stick of unsalted butter soften, parsley flakes, seasoned salt, pepper, garlic powder, paprika and 1 container of chicken broth.

Step 1. Pre-heat your oven to 350 degrees.
Clean your chicken with salt and water inside and outside.
Shake off the water. Take some paper towels and dry the chicken completely.

Step 2. The Ingredients
Cut your lemon in half. Peel your onion and cut it in half. Take two pieces of garlic and split it in half. Take about four pieces of thyme and stuff all of these ingredients inside of the chicken.

Step 3. Once your chicken is dry, take your butter and rub the chicken down the front, down the back and up under the skin. Take your seasonings and just sprinkle them all over your chicken. Pull about 1 ½ cup of chicken broth in the bottom of your pan, place the chicken in the pan and cover it with foil.

Step 4. After cooking for 1 hour and half take off the foil and baste the chicken. Leave in the oven and continue to cook for an additional hour and half.

Cook time ~ 3 hours.

For step by step instruction follow me on YouTube

Meat Loaf (Turkey or Beef ~2 in 1)

You will need

Ground Beef or Ground Turkey (your preference), 2 eggs, 1 cup of bread crumbs, mayonnaise, seasoned salt, pepper, garlic powder, onion powder, parsley flakes, ½ of green pepper (chopped), 1 whole onion (chopped).

Step 1. Place your meat in a bowl, 1 whole chopped onion, ½ chopped green pepper and all your seasonings. Then add 1/4 cup of mayonnaise, mix it all together and shape into a loaf.

Step 2. Place your loaf in a pan and place it in the oven at 350 degrees. Once your meat loaf is done add the barbecue sauce of choice. I prefer Sweet Baby Rays Honey. Place back in oven for an additional 10 to 15 minutes just to get the sauce hot.

Cook time ~ two hours or until done to your liking

For step by step instruction follow me on YouTube

Fried Fish

You will need

Fish of choice, all-purpose flour, cornmeal, pepper, seasoned salt and cooking oil.
My preference of fish is Tilapia and my choice of cooking oil is vegetable oil.

Step 1. Wash your fish off in warm water and pat dry with some paper towels. Place fish on a plate and season it with the season salt and pepper.

Step 2. Make the batter by using 1 cup of flour, 1 cup of cornmeal and some extra seasonings. Place the oil in the pan on medium heat to allow it to get hot.

Step 3. While the oil is getting hot, take your seasoned fish and place it in the batter, being sure to coat it. Shake off the excessive batter and place your fish one at a time in the pan with the hot oil. Depending on the size of your pan, you may be able to place 2, 3 or more.

Step 4. Let your fish brown on one side for about ten minutes or so and flip to let it brown on the other side. If you like a crispy, crunchy fish, let your fish fry a little while longer. Continue with these steps until all your fish is finish and enjoy!!

For step by step instruction follow me on YouTube

Crab Cake

You will need

16 oz. can of Crab Meat (claw or lump), 1 egg, mustard, mayonnaise, bread crumbs, pepper, old bay season, parsley flakes and vegetable oil.

Step 1. Place your crab meat in bowl along with your ingredients: 1 egg 2 tsp of mustard, 1/4 cup of mayonnaise, 1 cup of bread crumbs, 1 tsp of pepper, 1 tbsp. of old bay season, 2 tsp of parsley flakes and mix it all up well.

Step 2. Place about 1/2 cup of vegetable oil in pan and let it get hot. Place your crab cakes in the pan. Let them get brown on one side for about 4 to 5 minutes and then flip them over, so they can brown on that side. Remove them from the pan and continue cooking the other crab cakes until you are done.

For step by step instruction follow me on YouTube

Turkey Burger

You will need

Ground Turkey Meat, mayonnaise, pepper, parsley flakes, seasoned salt, garlic powder and onion powder.
Cheese and Bacon are optional

Step 1. Mix all your seasonings (pepper, parsley flakes, seasoned salt, garlic powder and onion powder) into the bowl with your ground turkey. Add 2 tablespoons of mayonnaise next and mix it all together.

Step 2. Make your patties and place in the frying pan to cook.

Step 3. Cook on both sides for 5-10 minutes.

Step 4. Choose your condiments for your burger and enjoy.

For step by step instruction follow me on YouTube

Fried Chicken

You will need

Chicken of choice, seasoned salt, parsley flakes, pepper, garlic powder, buttermilk, flour and vegetable oil.

Step 1. Clean chicken and pat your chicken dry. Season the chicken with the seasonings: seasoned salt, parsley flakes, pepper and garlic powder. Place your oil on the stove and let it get hot.

Step 2. Get two bowls (one for buttermilk and one for flour). In the first bowl, pour 2 cups of buttermilk in there. In the second bowl, place 2 cups of flour, the same seasonings you used to season the chicken and mix it altogether.

Step 3. Dip your chicken into the buttermilk, flipping it over and over for about a minute or two. Shake off chicken and then dip into the flour front and back shack off extra flour then place in frying pan. This chicken will cook on medium heat until golden brown then flip depending or the size of your chicken it may take longer to cook.

For step by step instruction follow me on YouTube

Spaghetti and Meat Sauce

You will need

Ground Beef, ½ green pepper, 1 container of mushrooms, ½ onion, 3 jars of spaghetti sauce of your choice, 1 pk of eckrich sausage, garlic powder, pepper, seasoned salt, onion powder, parsley flakes, spaghetti noodles, vegetable oil and olive oil.
Sugar is optional

Step 1. In a large pot, add water, salt and 3 tablespoon of vegetable oil.

Step 2. Add 5 tablespoons of vegetable oil in a pan and let it get hot. Then add in your veggies: green peppers, onions and mushrooms. Let your veggies cook down until they are soft. Then add in your sausage and cook for about 15 minutes or until the sausage are done.

Step 3. Once the veggies and sausage are done, please remove them from the heat.
Season your ground beef and cook it until it is completely done. Remove the ground beef from the heat and drain the grease off your meat. Then add your 3 jars of spaghetti sauce to your ground beef and vegetables. Mix well. By now, your water should have come to a boil. So, add your spaghetti noodles and cook for about 15 to 20 minutes or until the noodles are completely done. Drain the noodles, place them back in pot and add 1 tablespoon of olive oil to prevent the noodles from sticking together.

Step 4. To your spaghetti noodles, you will add your meat sauce and 1/3 cup of Sugar which is optional. Stir in your meat sauce mix and let it all simmer for about 10 to 15 minutes.

Serve with some warm garlic bread or cheesy garlic bread (check out my bread section for my homemade garlic bread)

For step by step instruction follow me on YouTube

Smothered Pork Chops

You will need

Pork Chops, 1 onion, 1 green pepper, season salt, garlic powder, onion powder, pepper, paprika, vegetable oil, flour.

Step 1. Make sure your pan is on a medium heat, place some oil in the frying pan and then your veggies. Stir the veggies and let them cook for 10 minutes. While the veggies are cooking, season your pork chops and flour with the seasonings. After you season your pork chops, place them in the seasoned flour to coat and shake off any extra flour. Then add your pork chops in the pan one at a time on top of your veggies. It will take about 5 to 10 minutes for the pork chops to turn golden brown and then flip to the other side to cook until all your chops are done.

Step 3. Once all you chops and veggies are done, remove them from pan. Drain some of the grease out of the pan but leave the drippings from the pork chops in pan. Along with the remainder of the grease. Add ½ stick of unsalted butter and 4 tablespoons of flour to the pan. Stir until it turns into a rue and then add 1 cup of water while still stirring until the mixture becomes thick. Add some seasonings according to your taste. If it is too thick, add a little water at a time until it reach the consistency that you want your gravy to be. Then add your chops and veggies into the gravy and plate your meal.

For step by step instruction follow me on YouTube

Fish Tacos

You will need

Olive oil, tomato, lettuce, old bay seasoning, pepper, relish, mayonnaise, ketchup, hot sauce and flour tortillas.
My preference of fish is cod because it is boneless and meaty.

Step 1. Pour some olive oil in your pan, so the fish won't stick. Season your fish front and back with old bay seasoning and pepper. Place your seasoned fish in the pan and let the fish cook for 5 minutes to get a nice golden crisp crust. Then flip it and let it cook for 5 minutes.

Step 2. On a low heat take your tortilla wrap and place on the open fire over the stove and let it crisp. This will only take a minute or two to crisp both sides. You must watch these closely because a quick turn to do something else will burn your tortilla.

Step 3. The Sauce
1 cup of mayonnaise, 3 tablespoons of ketchup, 1 tablespoon of hot sauce, 2 tablespoons of relish, 3 teaspoons of old bay seasoning.

You can build your tacos and eat.

For step by step instruction follow me on YouTube

Chicken and Rice

You will need

Boneless Skinless Chicken Thighs, ½ onion, pepper, seasoned salt, long grain rice, cream of mushroom soup and chicken broth.

Step 1. Clean your chicken. Then place it in a large pot with 1 cup of water and 2 cups of chicken broth along with your onions, seasoned salt and pepper. Let your chicken cook on a medium heat for 2 hours or until the chicken is falling apart.

Step 2. Once the chicken is done, add in your rice. If the water has boiled down add one cup of water to it and add more seasoning. Let the chicken and rice cook down on a low heat.

Step 3. Once the chicken and rice has cooked down, add in one can of cream of mushroom soup to give it a creamy texture. Let it cook for about 10 minutes and well your meal is ready to serve.

Smothered Chicken

You will need

Chicken, ½ onion, ½ green pepper, flour, olive oil, chicken broth, seasoned salt, black pepper, garlic powder, onion powder, parsley flakes, unsalted butter and vegetable oil.

Step 1. Clean and pat dry your chicken. Place the chicken in a large bowl, pour 4 tablespoons of olive oil all over it and rub it in. After that season your chicken with your seasonings: seasoned salt, black pepper, garlic powder, onion powder and parsley flakes. Cut up your vegetables: onion and green pepper and lay them in the baking dish. Place your chicken on top of your vegetables and pour the olive oil in the baking dish of each corner and in the middle area. Then cover with foil and place in the oven at 350 degrees for 1 hour and 30 minutes.

Step 2. After 1 hour and 30 minutes, take the foil off and flip your chicken. Drain some of the juice off but not a lot because you don't want the chicken to stick or burn. Place your chicken back in the oven and let it cook until it is golden crispy or as crispy as you like it. Then drain off the chicken juice into a bowl so that you can use it for the gravy.

Step 3. Making the gravy
In a pan, take a ½ stick of butter and let it melt along with 4 tablespoons of vegetable oil and 5 tablespoons of flour to make a rue. Once everything is mix well add in your chicken juice a little at a time while stirring it all over a low heat. Depending on how thick or thin you want your gravy, keep adding your juice. If you run out of juice, use the chicken broth. Once your gravy is the way that you like it, pour it over your chicken and mix it up.

Step 4. Place the chicken back in over for 5 to 10 minutes just to let the chicken and gravy come together. Your chicken is now done.

Serve with your favorite side dishes.

For step by step instruction follow me on YouTube

Pot Roast

You will need

Pot Roast, 5 diced potatoes, 3 carrots, ½ green pepper, ½ onion, flour, beef broth, seasoned salt and black pepper.

Step 1. Cut up your vegetables and set them aside. Then season your roast and rub it down with flour. Place your roast in the crockpot along with 2 cups of broth and 1 cup of water. Place it in the crockpot on low.

If using a baking dish, repeat steps and cover it with foil tightly. Place your roast in the oven on 250 degrees and let it cook.

Step 2. Let roast cook for 2 hours untouched. After the roast cook for 2 hours you should then flip it and in a small bowl add 2 tablespoons of flour and 2 teaspoons of water. Mix that well and add it to the roast juice to thicken it. Let it cook for another 2 hours. Your roast will been completely done, nice and tender.

Side Dishes

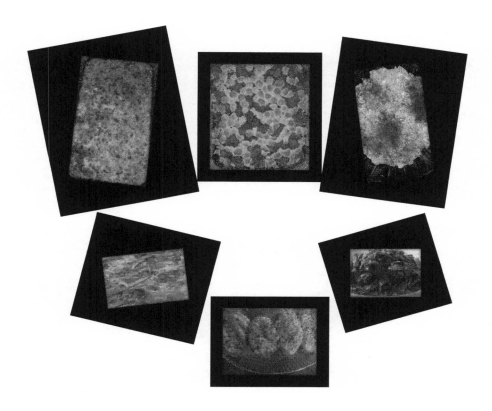

Potato Salad

You will need

5 Pounds of Potatoes, 1 green pepper, garlic powder, onion powder, mustard, mayonnaise, relish, 1 dozen of eggs, pepper.

Step 1. Place your potatoes in a pot of cold water. This will ensure that the potatoes cook evenly. Place your eggs in a pot of cold water and let them cook. Cook the potatoes until you can stick the fork through and they are tender. Drain the water and let the potatoes cool. Once cooled, peel your potatoes and cut them into small dices.

Step 2. Place your diced potatoes in a large bowl. Add in 2 tablespoons of mustard, 2 tablespoon of garlic powder, 2 tablespoon of onion powder and 2 teaspoons of pepper. Cut up your green pepper, add 1 cup of mayonnaise, 1/2 cup of relish drained (drain the juice off the relish), add 3 tablespoons of sugar (optional) and add your eggs. Using your hands or a large spoon, mix it up well.

Step 3. After you mix all your ingredients, taste to see if you need anything extra and just add seasonings some at a time and mix. Once your potatoes salad is to your liking (taste wise), sprinkle paprika on top and place it in refrigerator.

For step by step instruction follow me on YouTube

Green Beans

You will need

Green Beans, turkey smoked necks, onions, seasoned salted, unsalted butter.

Step 1. Clean and rinse off your string beans. Place them to the side.

Step 2. Place your turkey necks in a pot with water and place the pot on the stove on medium heat. Let the necks cook for at least one hour. Then add your seasoned salt and your green beans. Let it cook for 30 minutes. Cut your onion up into your string beans and stir. Add ½ stick of butter and keep your stove on a medium heat while your string beans cook down. Keep checking the water level to ensure that your green beans don't stick. The total cooking time for these green beans is 3 hours.

For step by step instruction follow me on YouTube

Macaroni and Cheese

You will need

16 oz. box of macaroni noodles, 1/2 cup of sour cream, 2 eggs, 2 cups of milk, 1 bag of shredded cheese, 1 bag of cheddar cheese, 1 block of Velveeta cheese spread, 1 block of sharp cheese, pepper, 2 tablespoons of sugar, vegetable oil.

Step 1. In a large pan, place water, salt and 1 tablespoon of vegetable oil on a medium heat. Let the water come to a boil and add your macaroni noodles. Noodles should cook for at least 20 to 30 minutes or until noodles are tender. Then drain the water off the noodles and place them into your baking dish.

Step 3. At this point, you will add 2 eggs mixed well, 1 cup of shredded cheese and 1 cup of cheddar cheese. Cut up your block sharp cheese and add it to the macaroni noodles and stir.

Step 4. Cheese sauce

Cut up your Velveeta cheese spread, add 1 cup of cheddar cheese, add 1 cup of shredded cheese add your 2 cups of milk on low heat. Let all you cheese melt together constantly stirring so it won't stick to pot.
Once the cheese is all melted together, pour over your macaroni noodles and stir. Then add your 2 tablespoons of sugar (optional), your sour cream and pepper. Mix well. With all your remaining cheese, sprinkle it over your macaroni and place it in the oven at 350 degrees for about 30 to 40 minutes.

For step by step instruction follow me on YouTube

Collard Greens

Your will need

Collard greens, seasoned salt, unsalted butter, onions and turkey necks or ham hocks, vinegar.

Step 1. Clean greens in a bid of warm water. Pull the greens off the stems and continue to clean with running water. Once the greens had a good rinse, place them in a bowl.

Step 2. Cook your turkey necks or ham hocks in pot of water with seasoned salt for 1 hour before adding your greens. After 1 hour, add your greens in with your meat. Let the greens cook an additional 2 hours and add more seasoned salt along with as much onions as you like and your stick of butter, 2 caps of Vinegar and mix it up letting the greens cook down for another hour. Keep checking on your greens. Taste them to see if anymore seasoning is needed. Once the greens are tender and seasoned to your liking, cut them off because they are done. The total time cooking collard greens is about 5 hours.

For step by step instruction follow me on YouTube

Candied Yams

You will need

Fresh yams or canned yams whichever, you prefer. Sugar, Brown sugar, unsalted butter, pure vanilla, cinnamon, nutmeg.

Step 1. Place yams in a pot of cold water, so that they will cook evenly. Let the yams cook on medium heat until they are tender. If you use can yams, drain the juice off the yams and place them in a baking dish.

Step 2. Candied Sauce- place 1 stick of butter in a pan along with ½ cup of brown sugar, ½ cup of sugar, 2 teaspoons of vanilla, 1 teaspoons of nutmeg and 1 tablespoon of cinnamon. Let the candied sauce melt down together. This will take 2 to 3 minutes.

Step 3. Once the sauce finished, pour the candied sauce all over your yams, sprinkle some brown sugar over the top and cover the yams. Place the yams in the oven on 350 degrees for 30 to 40 minutes. If you like marshmallows, you can add them on top of your yams.

For step by step instruction follow me on YouTube

<u>Cranberry Sauce</u>

You will need

One bag of cranberries, orange juice, cranberry juice, brown sugar, orange zest.

Step 1. Place your cranberries in pan along with ½ cup of orange juice, ½ cup of cranberry juice, ½ cup of brown sugar, and the zest of one orange. Let the cranberries simmer on a medium heat for 20 to 30 minutes. At this point, the cranberries will start to bust open and foam. Take a spoon and remove some of the foam.

Step 2. Stir and let the cranberries cook down to a jelly like texture. Once it's done, you can place your cranberries in a bowl, let them cool down, place a piece of plastic wrap over it and then put them in the refrigerator.

For step by step instruction follow me on YouTube

Scalloped Potatoes

You will need

Potatoes, milk, flour, onions, cheddar cheese, Velveeta cheese spread, unsalted butter.

Step 1. Peel your potatoes and cut them. Place your peeled potatoes in a pot of cold water with salt and let them boil on medium heat for 10 minutes. Then drain the water off the potatoes.

Step 2. For your cheese sauce, place ½ stick of butter in pan with your diced onions and let them cook for about 3 minutes. Then add 4 tablespoons of flour and stir until the flour has mixed well with the butter. At this point, add 2 cups of milk and stir for about 3 minutes or until it get thick. Add 3 cups of cheddar cheese, ½ block of the Velveeta cheese and turn the heat down to low while stirring it and allowing it to cook.

Step 3. Doing one layer at a time, place some of your potatoes in a baking pan and pull some cheese sauce over it. Layer again, potatoes and cheese sauce. When you reach your final layer, sprinkle cheddar cheese over the top of that layer potatoes. Cover with foil and place in the oven at 350 degrees for 30 minutes. In 30 minutes, remove the foil and let it cook for another 30 minutes. Then plate your meal.

For step by step instruction follow me on YouTube

Dressing with Sweet Italian Sausage

You will need

One bag of seasoned bread crumbs, poultry seasoning, unsalted butter, chicken broth, sweet Italian sausage, onions, celery, vegetable oil.

Step 1. In a pan, add 4 tablespoons of oil and let it get hot. Then add your onions and celery to the pan. Let your vegetables cook down for about 2-3 minutes. Once the veggies are cooked down, add your sausage and cook until sausage are done.

Step 2. Once the sausage are done, add in the bread crumbs, 2 cups of chicken broth, 2 tablespoon of poultry seasoning, and 1 tablespoon of sage. Stir everything all up together. If needed, add more chicken broth. Then place your dressing in a baking pan and bake it on 350 degrees for 15 minutes.

For step by step instruction follow me on YouTube

Twice Baked Potato

You will need

Four Large baked Potatoes, cheddar cheese, vegetable oil, sour cream, salt, black pepper, bacon, fresh parsley, unsalted butter, heavy cream.

Step 1. In a frying pan, cook 8 strips of bacon. While the bacon is cooking, you should clean your potatoes and put them aside after you pat them dry. Then take your potato and rub them down with some vegetable oil. Then place your potatoes in a baking dish in the oven at 375 degrees for about 1 hour.

Step 2. Take the potatoes out of the oven and let them cool. Once the potatoes are cooled, cut the potatoes down the middle and take a spoon to scoop out the inner part of the potatoes. Place the inner part of the potatoes in a large bowl. Once all the potatoes are spooned out, you should add in your chopped bacon, ½ cup of sour cream, salt, black pepper, 2 tablespoon of butter, ½ cup of heavy cream, fresh parsley chopped in small pieces and 1 cup of cheese. Using a potato masher or a hand mixer, combine all your ingredients.

Step 3. After you blend everything up, taste the filling to make sure it has enough seasoning. If everything is good, with a large spoon pick up your potato shell and scoop the filling into the shell. Once all the potato shells are filled, sprinkle extra cheese on top of the potatoes and place them back in the oven for 30 minutes. Remove and plate them. This is a terrific side dish that your family will enjoy.

Breakfast

Breakfast Croissant Quiche

You will need

2 packs of croissant rolls, 7 eggs, spinach, cheddar cheese, butter cooking spray, pepper, turkey meat, tomatoes and cupcake pan.

Step 1. Pre-heat the oven at the temperature that is on your croissant package. Spray your cupcake pan with butter spray. Open your croissants, pull them apart and place them into the cupcake pan using your finger to flatten them out. Repeat steps until all the cups are done.

Step 2. Egg filling. In a large bowl, add your 7 eggs, chopped spinach, cheese, black pepper and turkey meat. Mix well. Pour your egg filling into the cupcake pan but do not fill it to the top because you do not want it to overflow. Then place it in oven and let it cook for 15 to 20 minutes.

Step 3. Remove the pan. Take your fork to remove each mini quiche and place it on a plate. Enjoy!!

For step by step instruction follow me on YouTube

Buttermilk Waffles

You will need

Flour (all purpose or self-rising), baking powder, baking soda, salt, vegetable oil, sugar, butter milk, vanilla, waffle iron, eggs.

Step 1. In a large bowl, place all your dry ingredients: 2 cups of flour, 2 teaspoons of baking powder, 1 teaspoon of baking soda, 1 teaspoon of salt and 3 tablespoons of sugar. Mix it well and set it aside.

Step 2. In another bowl, place your wet ingredients: 2 eggs, 2 teaspoons of vanilla, 1 ½ cup of buttermilk and 3 tablespoons of oil. Mix well.

Step 3. Now, add your wet ingredients to your dry ingredients and mix. If the batter appears to be too thick, add more buttermilk a little at a time until it is the way you like it (not too thick but not too lose).

Step 4. Spray your waffle iron with the butter spray and then pour your waffle mix in it but do not overflow the iron. Most waffles irons come with a light to let you know the waffles are done. Just repeat this step until all the waffle mix is gone. Butter and serve.

For step by step instruction follow me on YouTube

Potato Melody

You will need

One bag of potatoes 5 pounds, green pepper, red peppers, onion, beef sausage, seasoned salt, garlic powder, onion powder, parsley flakes, black pepper, vegetable oil, cheddar cheese.

Step 1. Dice your potatoes place in bowl rinse off. Then mix in your seasonings and vegetables. Using a large frying pan add your 2 cups of oil, let the pan get hot and add in your potatoes. Let them cook until they are tender and golden brown. Then remove from pan and drain the grease.

Step 2. Cut your beef sausage up and cook them in a pan. Once the sausage is cooked, completely add them to your potatoes and mix well. Place the potato/sausage mixture in a baking pan and sprinkle cheddar cheese over the top. Put in the oven for 15 minutes or until cheese is melted. Remove from the oven and eat. Your family will enjoy this.

For step by step instruction follow me on YouTube

Shrimp and Grits

You will need

Grits, 20 shrimps peeled and deveined, onions, minced garlic, salt, black pepper, andouille sausage, unsalted butter, cheddar cheese, half and half, chicken broth.

Step 1. In a large frying pan, add 4 tablespoons of oil along with your onions. Stir and let it simmer down. Then add in a tablespoon of garlic and stir for about 2 minutes but do not allow it to burn. Add in your cut up sausage while stirring and let it cook for 5 minutes or until the sausage are done. Remove your sausage mix from stove and place it in a bowl. Rinse the frying pan. Put 2 tablespoons of butter in the frying pan. Then add in your shrimp along with salt and black pepper. The shrimp doesn't take long to cook. Therefore, cook it for about 3 to 4 minutes or until you see a change in the color of the shrimp (an orange color). Then add your sausage mix to the shrimp and stir it up.

Step 2. In a pot, add in 1 cup of chicken broth and let come to a boil. Then add in 1 cup of half and half and 2 tablespoons of butter. Once you add in the half and half, the temperature will drop. So, let everything come to a boil again and add in 1 ½ cup of grits while stirring. Watch your grits so they won't burn. When the grits are thick, you will need to add in 1 cup of cheese and mix well.

Step 3. Place your grits on a plate add your shrimp and sausage on top. Your meal is now complete. Enjoy.

For step by step instruction follow me on YouTube

Appetizers

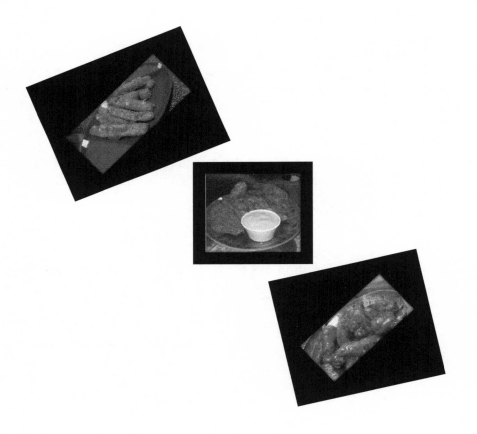

Mozzarella Cheese Sticks

You will need

One block of Mozzarella Cheese, Italian Bread Crumbs, Eggs, Flour, Vegetable oil, water.

Step 1. Cut your mozzarella cheese into long sticks like fries and place them all on a plate. Get 3 bowls out. First bowl~ add 2 cups of bread crumbs. Second bowl ~add 4 eggs and 2 teaspoons of water. 3rd bowl~ add flour.

Step 2. Take each cheese stick, one at a time. Coat them with your flour. Next your egg wash and shake off the extra eggs drippings. Last, coat it with your bread crumbs. After all the stick are covered, you will need to repeat the coating process (double coating) because it will help to keep the cheese firm.

Step 3. After double coating, place your cheese sticks in the freezer for 6 hours. If you have to use 2 plates, don't stack them on top of each other because you want them to freeze up nice and stiff. You can always make this dish the night before and just wrap plastic wrap over the plates of cheese sticks.

Step 4. After the 6 hours is up, pull one plate at a time out of the freezer to cook. In a pot you will need 4 cups of vegetable oil because you will be deep frying your cheese sticks. Let the pot get hot on a high heat. Once the grease is hot, place your cheese sticks in 4 to 5 at a time depending on how big your pot is. Let the stick get golden brown on one side then flip it. This should only take about 5 minutes to cook each batch of sticks. Once the first plate is done, pull your other plate out the freezer and cook those. Serve with your favorite marinara sauce.

For step by step instruction follow me on YouTube

Buffalo Wings

You will need

One bag of party wings, parsley flakes, hot sauce, unsalted butter, black pepper, seasoned salt, garlic powder, vegetable oil.

Step 1. Rinse and pat dry your chicken. Season it well and place on a dry plate. In a large pot, add vegetable oil because you will be deep frying your party wings. Once the oil is nice and hot, add in the chicken a batch at a time depending on the size of your pot. Let the chicken cook until crispy and flip repeatedly so that both sides of the chicken can cook. Remove your wings when they are done.

Step 2. In a frying pan, add 1 cup of hot sauce, a half stick of unsalted butter and 3 teaspoons of parsley flakes. Cook until the butter is melted down and then place your chicken into the buffalo sauce. Mix well and plate to serve.

If you like your wings hotter, use less butter. If you like your wings milder, use more butter. This is a great treat that your family will love!!!

For step by step instruction follow me on YouTube

Chicken Nuggets

You will need

Chicken breast, Italian bread crumbs, eggs, flour, vegetable oil, seasoning salt, black pepper.

Step 1. Clean your chicken breast, pat them dry, cut them into pieces and season them. Get some small bowls. First bowl, add the eggs with two teaspoon of water and mix. Next bowl, add your flour. Last bowl, add your bread crumbs.

Step 2. Take each piece of chicken and dunk into your flour first, shake it off. Next, dunk it into your egg wash and shake it off. Last, dunk it into the bread crumbs and then sit it aside until all pieces are completed.

Step 3. In a frying pan, heat up your oil on a medium high heat. Once the oil is nice and hot, add your nuggets one at a time. Let each piece cook until they are golden brown and then flip them. Repeat this process until all your nuggets are done and serve with your favorite dipping sauce.

Breads

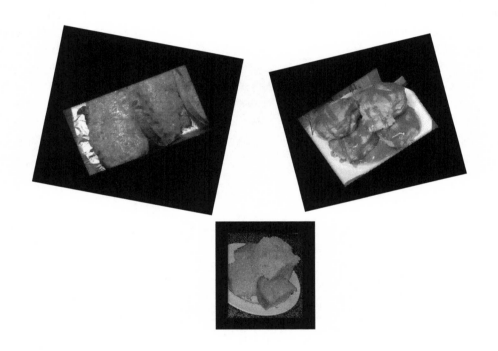

Scratch Cornbread

You will need

Yellow cornmeal, flour, baking powder, corn oil, unsalted butter, eggs butter milk, salt and sugar

Step 1. In a large bowl, add 1 cup of cornmeal, 1 cup of flour, 2 teaspoon of baking powder, 1 teaspoon of salt, 2 eggs, ½ cup of sugar, 3 tablespoons of corn oil and 1 ½ cup of buttermilk. Mix well.

Step 2. Melt ½ stick of butter and pour only 1 tablespoon of butter into your batter. Mix that up. Using the rest of your melted butter, grease your baking pan. Pour your cornbread batter into your baking pan and place it in the oven on 400 degrees for 30 minutes or until the center of the cornbread is no longer loose and the cornbread is golden brown.

Step 3. Once the cornbread is done, remove it from the oven and rub butter across top. If you like to, you could also put honey on top and serve warm.

For step by step instruction follow me on YouTube

Homemade Buttermilk Biscuits

You will need

Self- rising flour, unsalted butter, salt, butter milk, sugar, rolling pin, biscuit cutter.

Step 1. In a large bowl, add 3 cups of flour, 1 teaspoon of salt, 5 tablespoons of sugar, and 2 sticks of unsalted butter (cut into pieces). Using your hands, crumble everything together.

Step 2. Once the flour is crumbled together, add in your buttermilk a tablespoon at a time starting with 3 tablespoons. Using your hands, mix the buttermilk into the flour mix until it pulls away from the bowl. Adding 2 more tablespoons of buttermilk at this point, you should have a ball of dough.

Step 3. Flour your counter top with some flour. Place your dough on to the top and fold the dough over and over again at least 4 to 5 times. Take some flour and rub your rolling pin up and down. Start to roll your dough out with the rolling pin and begin to cut out your biscuits.

Step 4. Place your biscuits onto a baking sheet, then melt some butter. Using a pastry brush, rub butter onto the biscuits and place them in the oven on 425 degrees for about 12 minutes or until they are golden brown.

For step by step instruction follow me on YouTube

Homemade Garlic Bread

You will need

1bag of sub rolls, 1 stick of unsalted butter (room temperature),
½ cup of mozzarella cheese, ½ cup of cheddar cheese and 2 tsp of parsley flakes, 1 cup of mayonnaise, 3 tsp of garlic powder

Step 1. In a bowl, you will mix your mayonnaise, cheeses, parsley flakes, garlic powder and the room temperature butter.

Step 2. Take your rolls, cut them in half and spread your mix directly onto the bread

Step 3. Once you have finished spreading the mix on the bread, sprinkle more cheese on the bread and place it in the oven on broil until they are golden brown.

For step by step instruction follow me on YouTube

Cocktails

Mac Lovin' Juice

You will need

A bottle of your best Vodka, Passion Fruit Malibu Rum, frozen strawberries, frozen pineapples, 2 liter of ginger ale, simply lemonade raspberry, ice.

Step 1. In a large jug or pitcher add you all fruits the whole bottle of ginger ale, the whole lemonade and ice and mix well.

Step 2. Add in your Vodka and Malibu Rum in some at a time making it as strong or mild as you like it. It's all about taste.

Green Machine (makes 2 jugs)

You will need

2 empty gallon jugs, ½ gallon of Apple Vodka (your choice), 2 big (64oz) everfresh lime juices or 6 small (8oz) everfresh lime juices, 4 small everfresh cranberry juice, and a glass of ice chilled and garnished with a wedge slice of granny smith apple.

Step 1. Take your granny smith apple and rinse it off with cold water. Cut it in half and then cut the half in half vertically. Take your wedges, cut a slit in the middle and put it aside.

Step 2. Take your glass or glasses and fill them with ice. Take your apple wedges, place them on the rim of your glass and then put your glass in the freezer to chill.

Step 3. Take 2- empty gallon jugs and add half of your ½ a gallon of apple vodka to each.

Step 4. Take your lime juice and pour 1 big bottle or 3 smaller bottles in each jug.

Step 5. Take your 4 small cranberry juices and pour 2 in each jug.

Step 6. Shake, Shake and Shake.

Step 7. Take your glasses out of the freezer, pour your mix and serve.

You can also mix this in a pitcher, cooler or a punch bowl.

Mango Madness (makes 2 jugs)

You will need

2 empty gallon jugs, ½ gallon of Mango Vodka (your choice), 2 big (64oz) everfresh lime juices or 4 small (8oz) everfresh lime juices, 4 small everfresh cranberry juice, 4 small everfresh mango juice and a glass of ice chilled and garnished with frozen or fresh mangos.

Step 1. Take fresh or frozen mangos out. Cut the fresh ones after rinsing and peeling. Place them in a bowl. If frozen, place them in a bowl and put aside.

Step 2. Take your glass or glasses and fill them with ice and put your glass in the freezer to chill.

Step 3. Take 2- empty gallon jugs and add half of your ½ a gallon of mango vodka to each.

Step 4. Take your lime juice and pour 1 big bottle or 2 smaller bottles in each jug.

Step 5. Take your 4 small cranberry juices and pour 2 in each jug.

Step 6. Take your 4 small mango juices and pour 2 in each jug.

Step 7. Shake, Shake and Shake.

Step 8. Take your glasses out of the freezer, pour your mix, put a couple of mangos in there and serve.

You can also mix this in a pitcher, cooler or a punch bowl.

Jammie Jam Jello

You will need

Small plastic container cups with lids, 2 packs of Jell-O brand Jell-O (any flavor), water, Vodka (cold)

Step 1. Take your Jell-O and empty in a bowl and put aside.

Step 2. Boil water in a pot. Take 2 cups of boiled water and empty it in the Jell-O. Mix it up really go.

Step 3. Take 2 cups of cold vodka and empty it into the bowl with the mix and stir.

Step 4. Take your mix and pull it in the plastic containers one at a time. Place the lids on them and put them in the refrigerator until they are gelled.

This Book is dedicated to my family, friends and all my YouTube subscribers. Thank you all so much for the love and support. I hope you all enjoyed all of these soulful homemade recipes.

Sincerely,

Soulfult

Made in the USA
Middletown, DE
03 June 2017